A kitten to keep

Mary was very fond of animals. She wanted to have a pet at home but her mother would not let her. So Mary looked after the hamsters at school and wished that she could take them home. She liked to hold them in her hands and stroke their fur. She liked to look at their eyes and their funny little paws.

One day when Mary was going home from school she saw something lying at the side of the road. It was small and dark and round. She bent down and found that it was a black kitten.

She picked the kitten up and saw that it had been hurt. Its leg was bleeding. It lay very still in her hand. But it was warm, and she could feel its heart beating, so she knew that it was not dead.

Mary did not know what to do. She wanted to keep the kitten and look after it but she was sure that her mother would not let her.

Mary needed to find a place where she could keep the kitten without telling her mother. She wondered what she could do and she thought about her Gran.

Mary's Gran lived in a house with a garden and the garden had a shed in it. Gran was old and she was not very well. She needed a stick for walking and she did not often leave the house.

The garden was in a mess because Gran could not look after it. Sometimes Mary's mum went to cut the grass for her, but she did not like weeding, so the weeds grew everywhere.

Mary put the kitten in her schoolbag and she ran to her Gran's house. Her Gran was always glad to see her.

"Gran," said Mary, "I can weed your garden for you."

Gran was very pleased.
"You are a good girl," she said.

Mary went into the garden and opened the shed. She took the kitten out of her schoolbag and laid it on an old sack on the floor.

She pulled out some weeds. Then she ran into the house again.

"Gran," she said, "I'm thirsty. Can I have a drink, please?"

"Yes, of course you can," said Gran. "Help yourself, Mary."

Mary put some water in a glass and she put some milk in a cup. Gran was in another room. She wasn't watching.

Mary went into the garden again. She dipped her handkerchief into the water and she bathed the kitten's leg. Then she poured some milk into a saucer, but the kitten would not drink. So Mary dipped her finger in the milk and put it in the kitten's mouth. The kitten sucked her finger.

Mary pulled out some more weeds. Then she gave the kitten some more milk. Then she pulled out some more weeds. She had to leave the kitten at last, lying on the sack with the saucer of milk close beside it. She hoped it would not be cold during the night.

"Thank you, Mary," said Gran. "You are a good girl."

Mary said she would come back in the morning on her way to school. And she went home.

After Mary had gone, Gran sat thinking. "Mary is a good girl," she thought. "But why is she coming back in the morning? That's funny, that is!"

Mary got up early and ate her breakfast very quickly.

"Why are you in such a hurry today?" said her mum.

"I'm going to see Gran," said Mary. "I'm going to weed her garden."

"Before school?" said her mum. She thought that was funny.

Mary ran to her Gran's house. She went into the garden and opened the shed. The kitten was still lying on the sack. Mary picked it up and put the saucer of milk under its nose. The kitten began to lap the milk up and Mary was very pleased. When it stopped drinking she looked at the leg which had been bleeding. It was not bleeding now and the kitten could stand on it.

Suddenly Mary heard a noise behind her. She turned and saw Gran standing in the doorway.

"What are you doing Mary?" said Gran.

So Mary had to tell her Gran all about the kitten. She told Gran where she had found it. She said she was afraid to take it home because she knew her mum would not let her keep it.

"I want to keep it, Gran," she said. "It's mine now. I can't give it away."

Gran took Mary and the kitten into the house. They found a box and they put some rags in it for the kitten to lie on.

Then Gran said:

"We must try to find the owner of this kitten, Mary. But if we can't do that, I'll keep the kitten here for you and you can come every day to see it and look after it. Would you like that?"

Mary nodded. She hoped they would never find the owner, and they never did.

Mary went every day to Gran's house to look after the kitten. And she did not forget to weed the garden sometimes too!

Do you know?

Do you know what an **iceberg** is? An iceberg is a huge lump of ice floating in the sea.

Some lands are covered with ice and snow. Big lumps of ice break off and fall into the sea, and float about.

Icebergs are dangerous for ships, because you only see a small part of the ice above the water. All the rest is below the surface and it can have sharp edges sticking out.

Modern ships have radar to warn them when they are near an iceberg.

Tails

Nearly all animals have tails.
Horses have tails.
Pigs have tails.
So do elephants.
So do hamsters.

Birds have tails too.
Some birds have
beautiful, coloured tails.
These tails usually belong to
the male birds.
The female birds
have ordinary tails.

The peacock's tail
is very special.
Sometimes he walks
with it on the ground.
Sometimes he shows
off his beautiful tail
to the pea-hen.

Animals find their tails useful.

Cows use them
to swish away the flies.

Squirrels use their bushy tails
to keep them warm
in the winter.

Some monkeys use their tails
to twist round
the branches of trees
so that they can't fall.

We can tell
when a dog is pleased
to see us.
It wags its tail.
When a dog is not happy
its tail hangs down.

Do you know?

Do you know how blind people read books? They cannot see words in books like this. They have a different kind of book and they read in a different way. They read with their fingers.

Their books are written with a sharp point like a needle. The pricks make little bumps on the paper. Blind people read by feeling the bumps. Blind people learn what the bumps mean when they learn to read.

This way of reading and writing is called **Braille,** because a man named Louis Braille invented it.

a b c d e f g h i

Rumpelstiltskin

Once upon a time there was a miller who had a beautiful daughter. He loved her very much, and he was always telling people about her. He told them she was like the sun and the moon and the stars and the flowers. He told them about the clever things she could do.

13

One day the King came to the village where the miller lived, and the miller told the King about his daughter.

"She is very, very clever," he said. "She can take some straw and spin it, and turn it into threads of gold."

The King was very interested and he wanted to know if the miller was telling the truth.

"Bring her to the palace," he said.

So the miller took his daughter to the palace, and the King took her into a room that was full of straw. A servant brought a spinning-wheel.

"Spin the straw into gold," he told her. "If you haven't turned it all into gold before morning you will die."

When the girl was alone in the room, she began to weep.

"Why does my father say these silly things about me?" she sobbed. "I can't turn straw into gold. What am I to do?"

Suddenly she looked up and saw that a dwarf was standing in the room.

"Don't worry," he said. "I know how to turn straw into gold. What will you give me if I do it for you?"

"I'll give you my bracelet," said the girl, and the dwarf agreed. He began to spin, and soon all the straw was turned into threads of gold.

In the morning the King was delighted. "You must do the same thing again tonight," he said. "And then I shall marry you and you will be the Queen."

17

That night the King left the girl in another room full of straw, and the dwarf came once again.

"What will you give me if I help you?" he asked. But the girl had nothing else to give him.

"What can I do?" she cried, weeping.

"Don't worry," said the dwarf. "I know what to do. When you are the Queen, you will have a baby. You can give the baby to me."

The girl agreed, but she did not worry because she did not think that the King would keep his promise and marry her.

The dwarf sat down to spin for the second time. The King was delighted when he saw all the gold in the morning. He kept his promise and he married the beautiful girl.

After a year they had a son. The Queen loved her son very much. She had forgotten all about her promise by this time. But one evening, when she was alone, she suddenly saw the dwarf standing beside her.

19

"Give me your baby," said the dwarf. "Remember what you promised."

The Queen was horrified.

"You can take everything else that I have," she cried, "but not my baby!"

"It's the baby I want," the dwarf told her.

The Queen wept and wept and at last the dwarf said:

"I'll give you one more chance. If you can tell me my name you can keep the baby. I'll give you three days, that's all."

The next night the dwarf came back. The Queen tried a long list of names but they were all wrong.

The next night the dwarf was back again. The Queen had spent all day thinking of names but every one was wrong.

"You'll never guess it!" cried the dwarf. He laughed and disappeared.

Next day the Queen sent a page boy into town to ask people for all the names they knew. She told the page boy to write them all down and bring her the list before night-time.

On the way back to the palace the page boy walked through the forest and suddenly he heard a voice singing. He hid behind a tree and saw a dwarf dancing round and round, singing this song:

"I'm going to take the baby prince,
He will be mine tonight.
My name is *Rumpelstiltskin*,
But the Queen won't guess it right!"

When the page boy told the Queen what he had heard she laughed for joy.

"My baby is safe now!" she cried.

That night the dwarf came again.

"Is your name Rupert?" she asked.

"No," said the dwarf, rubbing his hands.

"Is it Renaldo?" she asked.

"No, no!" he shouted.

"Is it . . . *Rumpelstiltskin*?" said the Queen.

As soon as the dwarf heard his name he shrieked and disappeared in a cloud of grey smoke.

Nobody ever saw him again and everyone in the palace lived happily ever after.